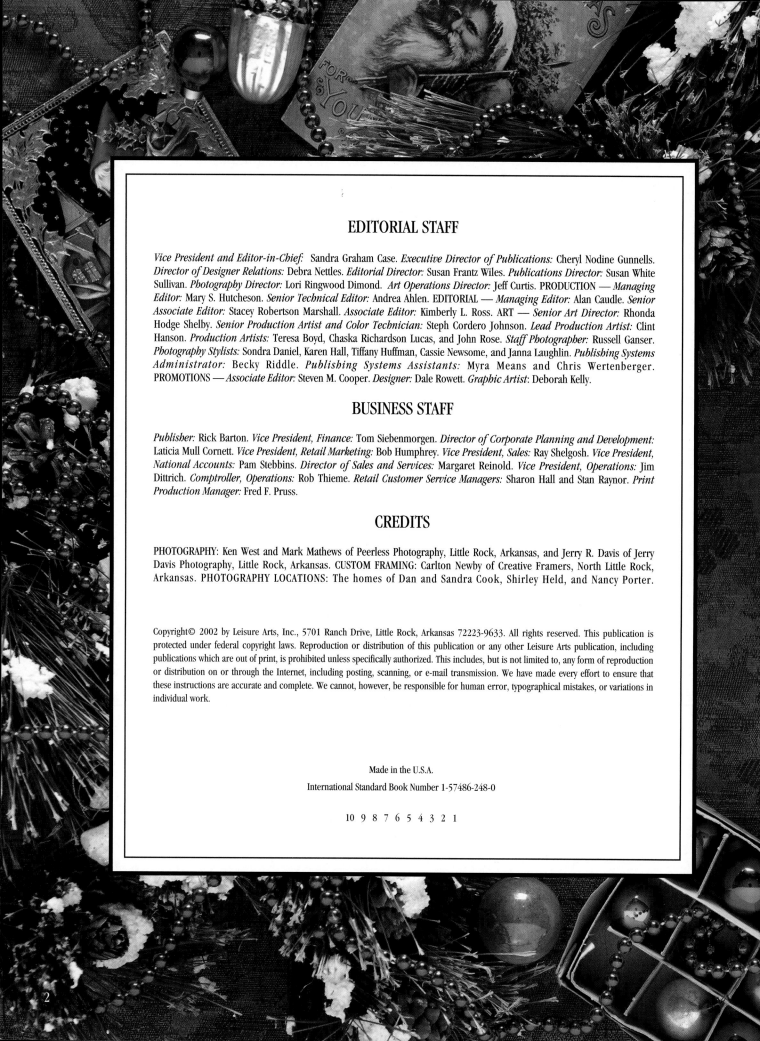

EDITORIAL STAFF

Vice President and Editor-in-Chief: Sandra Graham Case. *Executive Director of Publications:* Cheryl Nodine Gunnells. *Director of Designer Relations:* Debra Nettles. *Editorial Director:* Susan Frantz Wiles. *Publications Director:* Susan White Sullivan. *Photography Director:* Lori Ringwood Dimond. *Art Operations Director:* Jeff Curtis. PRODUCTION — *Managing Editor:* Mary S. Hutcheson. *Senior Technical Editor:* Andrea Ahlen. EDITORIAL — *Managing Editor:* Alan Caudle. *Senior Associate Editor:* Stacey Robertson Marshall. *Associate Editor:* Kimberly L. Ross. ART — *Senior Art Director:* Rhonda Hodge Shelby. *Senior Production Artist and Color Technician:* Steph Cordero Johnson. *Lead Production Artist:* Clint Hanson. *Production Artists:* Teresa Boyd, Chaska Richardson Lucas, and John Rose. *Staff Photographer:* Russell Ganser. *Photography Stylists:* Sondra Daniel, Karen Hall, Tiffany Huffman, Cassie Newsome, and Janna Laughlin. *Publishing Systems Administrator:* Becky Riddle. *Publishing Systems Assistants:* Myra Means and Chris Wertenberger. PROMOTIONS — *Associate Editor:* Steven M. Cooper. *Designer:* Dale Rowett. *Graphic Artist:* Deborah Kelly.

BUSINESS STAFF

Publisher: Rick Barton. *Vice President, Finance:* Tom Siebenmorgen. *Director of Corporate Planning and Development:* Laticia Mull Cornett. *Vice President, Retail Marketing:* Bob Humphrey. *Vice President, Sales:* Ray Shelgosh. *Vice President, National Accounts:* Pam Stebbins. *Director of Sales and Services:* Margaret Reinold. *Vice President, Operations:* Jim Dittrich. *Comptroller, Operations:* Rob Thieme. *Retail Customer Service Managers:* Sharon Hall and Stan Raynor. *Print Production Manager:* Fred F. Pruss.

CREDITS

PHOTOGRAPHY: Ken West and Mark Mathews of Peerless Photography, Little Rock, Arkansas, and Jerry R. Davis of Jerry Davis Photography, Little Rock, Arkansas. CUSTOM FRAMING: Carlton Newby of Creative Framers, North Little Rock, Arkansas. PHOTOGRAPHY LOCATIONS: The homes of Dan and Sandra Cook, Shirley Held, and Nancy Porter.

Made in the U.S.A.

International Standard Book Number 1-57486-248-0

10 9 8 7 6 5 4 3 2 1

INTRODUCTION

*O*h, how we love the glorious season of Christmas!
The simple joys of snowy days, family gatherings,
and gift-giving become wonderful memories that grow
more precious as the years go by. This new collection
of resplendent Yuletide projects will provide you with
hours of enjoyment as you stitch magnificent pieces
for loved ones or as your own holiday decorations.
Within these pages, you'll find exquisite angels,
precious children, handsome Santas, and elegant
flowers. Your mantel will become a showplace for
a rich angel stocking adorned with poinsettias …
the tree will come alive with brilliant "stained glass"
ornaments. A gorgeous Santa bell pull and throw pillow
become perfect presents, and our adorable snow babies
will touch the hearts of young and old alike. With so
much Christmas giving and decorating to do, you'll
want to stitch each and every one. May the beauty
of these heartwarming heirlooms bring joy to
you and yours throughout each holiday season.

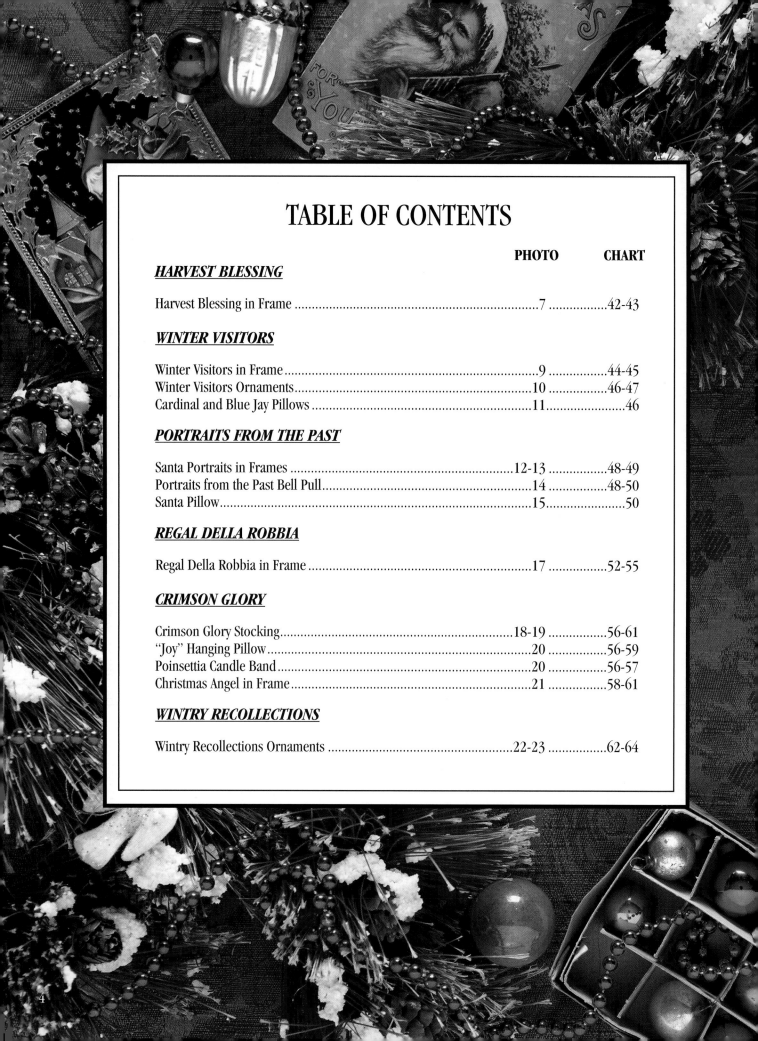

TABLE OF CONTENTS

	PHOTO	CHART

HARVEST BLESSING

Harvest Blessing in Frame 7 42-43

WINTER VISITORS

Winter Visitors in Frame 9 44-45
Winter Visitors Ornaments..10 46-47
Cardinal and Blue Jay Pillows...11.................46

PORTRAITS FROM THE PAST

Santa Portraits in Frames 12-13 48-49
Portraits from the Past Bell Pull...14 48-50
Santa Pillow...15.................50

REGAL DELLA ROBBIA

Regal Della Robbia in Frame 17 52-55

CRIMSON GLORY

Crimson Glory Stocking...18-19 56-61
"Joy" Hanging Pillow 20 56-59
Poinsettia Candle Band..20 56-57
Christmas Angel in Frame 21 58-61

WINTRY RECOLLECTIONS

Wintry Recollections Ornaments 22-23 62-64

	PHOTO	CHART

VISIONS OF OLDE ST. NICK

Visions of Olde St. Nick Stocking..24-25 68-73
St. Nick's Visit in Frame ....26.......................76
Santa and Sleigh in Frame ....27.......................68
Santa Standing Figure ....28...............74-75
Santa Ornament ....29...............70-73
St. Nicholas in Frame ....29...............68-71

ANGELS REJOICING

Angels Rejoicing Ornaments ....30-31................78-81

FATHER CHRISTMAS

Father Christmas in Frame 33 82-85

PLAYFUL SNOW BABIES

Playful Snow Babies in Frame 34-35 86-89
Playful Snow Babies Ornaments 36-37 86-89

O NIGHT DIVINE

O Night Divine Ornaments...38-39 65-67

SANTA'S FOREST FRIENDS

Santa's Forest Friends in Frame..41 90-93

General Instructions...96

HARVEST BLESSING

A time for recounting the many blessings we've received, Thanksgiving leads us into the Christmas celebration with grateful hearts. Greet this plentiful season with a nostalgic sampler perfect for display throughout the harvest months or all year round. Personalized with the stitcher's name, this heartwarming heirloom will be cherished by generations to come.

Chart on pages 42-43

WINTER VISITORS

Leaving tiny footprints in the snow, a troupe of feathered friends searches the snow-blanketed earth for its next hidden feast. This vibrant portrait of winged creatures makes a naturally beautiful addition to your holiday home.

Chart on pages 48-49

12

PORTRAITS FROM THE PAST

Whether we imagine him dressed in cheerful red or humble brown, Santa touches the hearts of everyone with his expressive face and soulful eyes. We take much delight in the many portraits of him that have been created through the ages.

Hope, love, peace, and faith
— these are just a few of the
heartfelt wishes that Santa
delivers to all the world each
year. As the guardian of
Christmas, he represents the
universal longing for peace on
earth and goodwill toward
our fellow man.

So remember, while December
Brings the Christmas day,
In the year let there be Christmas
In the things you do and say;
Wouldn't life be worth the living
Wouldn't dreams be coming true
If we kept the Christmas spirit
All the whole year through?

— ANONYMOUS

Chart on pages 48-50

14

Undeterred by whirling snow, this benevolent saint is
determined to complete his annual winter journey. His
eyes are fixed on the path before him, and his flowing
beard hides his kindly smile as he anticipates the joyous
greetings of good little children on his route.

Chart on page 50

REGAL
DELLA ROBBIA

Filled with the rich fruits of the earth, this resplendent wreath makes an opulent addition to your Yuletide décor, but you can also use it as a versatile accent throughout the year. Richly hued in the naturally beautiful colors of pomegranates, plums, grapes, and more, our ribbon-tied wreath is a wonderful gift idea for someone dear.

Chart on pages 52-55

Charts on pages 62-64

WINTRY RECOLLECTIONS

Capture a bit of the good old days with a nostalgic collection of Christmas ornaments. Miniature wintertime vignettes look like snapshots from a simpler time, when families traveled by horse and buggy and windows were aglow with candlelight. This assortment of old-fashioned trimmings is a splendid way to bring cheerful spirit to your home, whether you hang them on the evergreen or use them as distinctive gift embellishments.

Chart on pages 68-73

24

VISIONS OF
OLDE ST. NICK

Santa Claus is imagined in many ways
around the world, as depicted in this assortment
of wonderful gifts and decorations honoring
the jolly old elf. Framed pieces, ornaments,
and a freestanding figure will bring
the spirit of Saint Nicholas to young and
old alike for many Christmases to come.

ANGELS REJOICING

In lustrous gowns of pink and blue,
cheerful angels frolic among frost-tipped branches
and pearly spheres on this wreath of ornaments.
The captivating seraphs carry tiny treasures
of poinsettias and evergreens, and serve as lovely
tributes to the angels among us during
the holiday season.

Charts on pages 78-81

FATHER CHRISTMAS

As snowflakes gently fall on his crimson cloak, Father Christmas makes his monumental journey across the frozen land. Accompanied by his little woodland friends, the kindly gentleman promises to leave behind wondrous treasures for all the good little girls and boys he encounters along the way.

Chart on pages 82-85

33

SANTA'S FOREST FRIENDS

A to-be-treasured heirloom for generations to come, this cross-stitched masterpiece captures the kindhearted essence of everyone's favorite benevolent gent. Warm and toasty in his furry crimson coat, Santa Claus pauses to spend a quiet moment with his wee forest friends. A pleasure to stitch, our timeless portrait will bring the magic of Christmas into your home and heart.

Chart on pages 90-93

harvest blessing

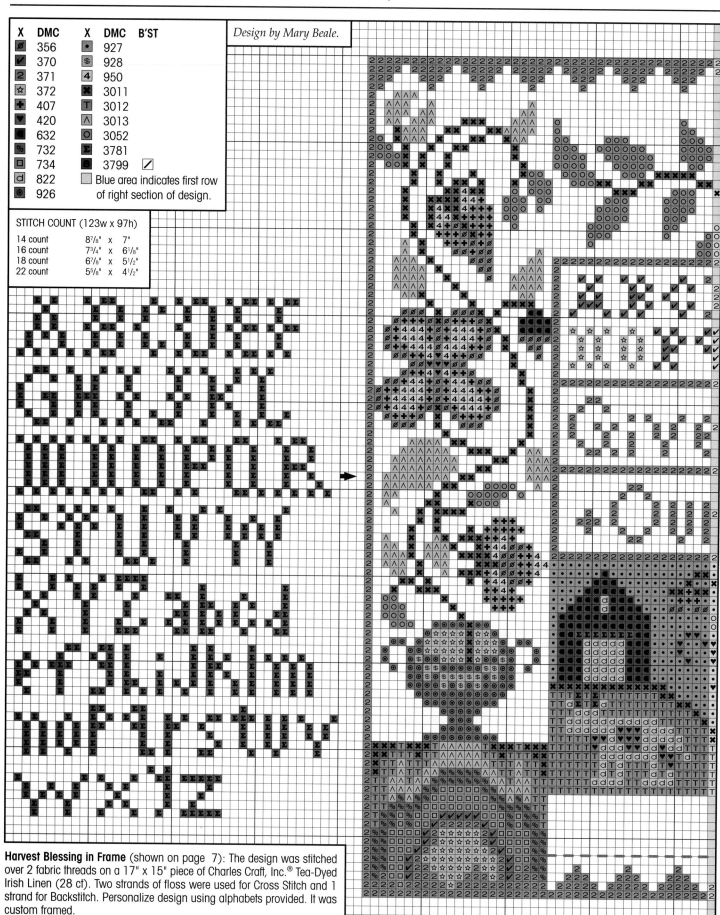

X	DMC	X	DMC	B'ST
⌀	356	•	927	
✔	370	$	928	
2	371	4	950	
☆	372	✖	3011	
✚	407	T	3012	
▼	420	∧	3013	
■	632	⊙	3052	
%	732	Σ	3781	
□	734	⊗	3799	╱
d	822			
⊙	926	Blue area indicates first row of right section of design.		

Design by Mary Beale.

STITCH COUNT (123w x 97h)

14 count	8⅞"	x	7"	
16 count	7¾"	x	6⅛"	
18 count	6⅞"	x	5½"	
22 count	5⅝"	x	4½"	

Harvest Blessing in Frame (shown on page 7): The design was stitched over 2 fabric threads on a 17" x 15" piece of Charles Craft, Inc.® Tea-Dyed Irish Linen (28 ct). Two strands of floss were used for Cross Stitch and 1 strand for Backstitch. Personalize design using alphabets provided. It was custom framed.

center name

WINTER VISITORS

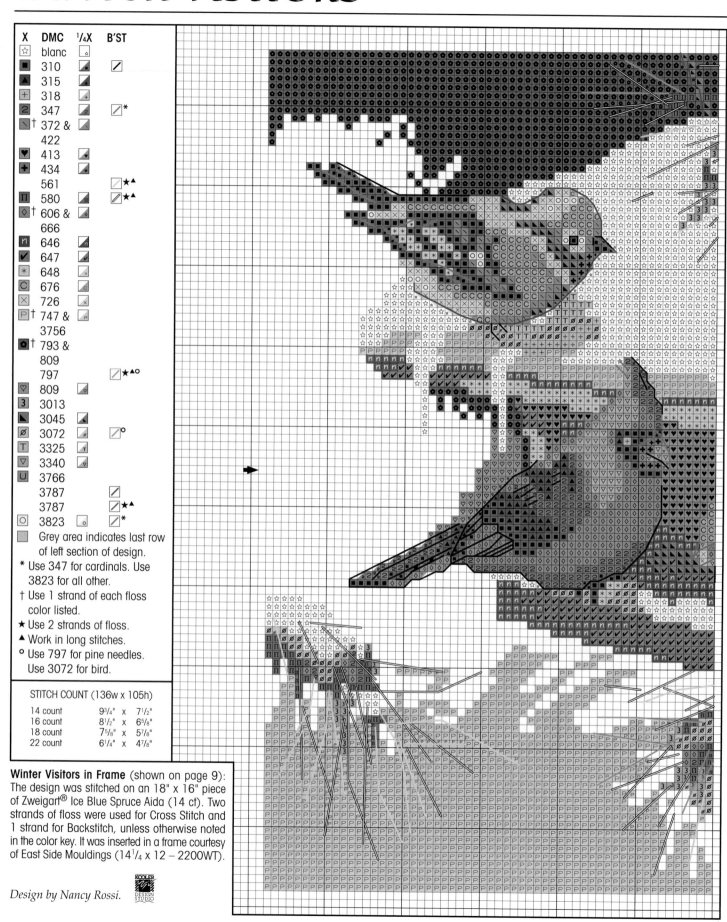

X	DMC	1/4X	B'ST
☆	blanc	☆	
■	310	◢	╱
▲	315	◢	
+	318	+	
2	347	2	╱ *
◨ †	372 &	◢	
	422		
♥	413	◢	
+	434	◢	
	561		╱ ★▲
Π	580	Π	╱ ★▲
◇ †	606 &	◢	
	666		
n	646	◢	
✔	647	◢	
✳	648	◢	
C	676	C	
✕	726	✕	
P †	747 &	P	
	3756		
◙ †	793 &	◢	
	809		
	797		╱ ★▲○
♥	809	◢	
3	3013	◢	
◣	3045	◢	
∅	3072	∅	╱ ○
T	3325	T	
▽	3340	◢	
U	3766		
	3787		╱
	3787		╱ ★▲
○	3823	○	╱ *

☐ Grey area indicates last row of left section of design.

* Use 347 for cardinals. Use 3823 for all other.

† Use 1 strand of each floss color listed.

★ Use 2 strands of floss.

▲ Work in long stitches.

○ Use 797 for pine needles. Use 3072 for bird.

STITCH COUNT (136w x 105h)

14 count	9¾"	x	7½"
16 count	8½"	x	6⅝"
18 count	7⅝"	x	5⅞"
22 count	6¼"	x	4⅞"

Winter Visitors in Frame (shown on page 9): The design was stitched on an 18" x 16" piece of Zweigart® Ice Blue Spruce Aida (14 ct). Two strands of floss were used for Cross Stitch and 1 strand for Backstitch, unless otherwise noted in the color key. It was inserted in a frame courtesy of East Side Mouldings (14¼ x 12 – 2200WT).

Design by Nancy Rossi.

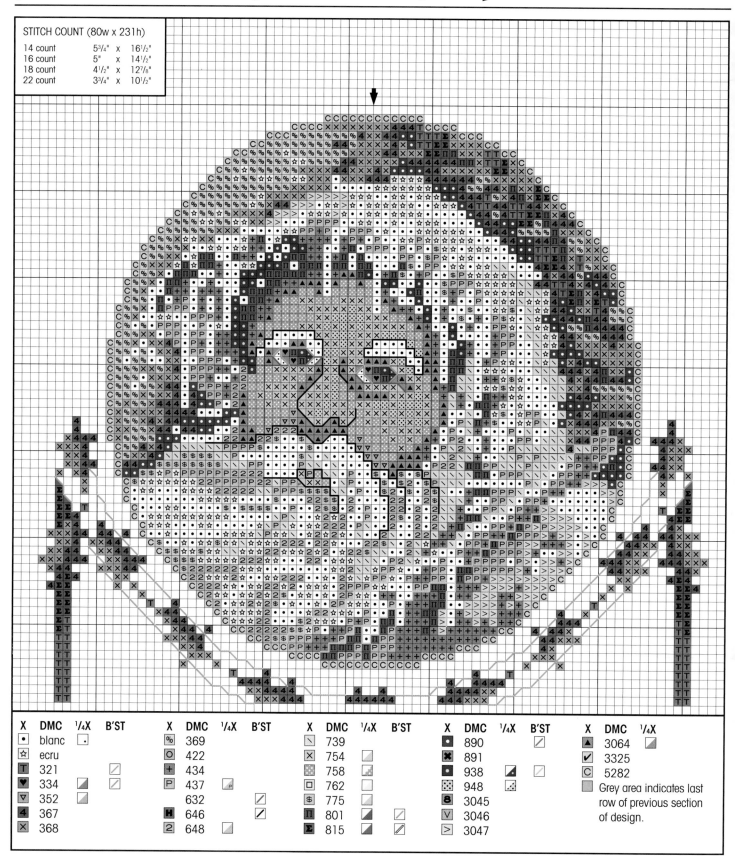

STITCH COUNT (80w x 231h)			
14 count	5¾"	x	16½"
16 count	5"	x	14½"
18 count	4½"	x	12⅞"
22 count	3¾"	x	10½"

X	DMC	¼X	B'ST		X	DMC	¼X	B'ST		X	DMC	¼X	B'ST		X	DMC	¼X	B'ST		X	DMC	¼X
•	blanc	•			%	369				\	739				◨	890		/		▲	3064	/
☆	ecru				O	422				X	754	/			✖	891				✔	3325	
T	321		/		+	434				▦	758	▨			◪	938	/	/		C	5282	
♥	334	◿	/		P	437	◿ₚ			▢	762				⦂	948	⦂					
▽	352	◿				632		/		$	775				8	3045				Grey area indicates last		
4	367				H	646		/		Π	801	/	/		V	3046				row of previous section		
✕	368				2	648	◿			Σ	815	/	/		>	3047				of design.		

Portraits from the Past Bell Pull (shown on page 14): The design was stitched over 2 fabric threads on a 14" x 25" piece of Zweigart® Antique White Cashel Linen® (28 ct). Two strands of floss were used for Cross Stitch and 1 strand for Backstitch. To complete bell pull, see Finishing Instructions, page 51.

Santa Portraits in Frames (shown on pages 12-13): Portions of the design (refer to photo) were each stitched over 2 fabric threads on a 14" square of Zweigart® Antique White Lugana (25 ct). Three strands of floss were used for Cross Stitch and 1 strand for Backstitch. They were custom framed.

Santa Pillow (shown on page 15): A portion of the design (refer to photo) was stitched over 2 fabric threads on a 12" square of Zweigart® Antique White Cashel Linen® (28 ct). Two strands of floss were used for Cross Stitch and 1 strand for Backstitch. To complete pillow, see Finishing Instructions, page 51.

Design by Donna Vermillion Giampa.

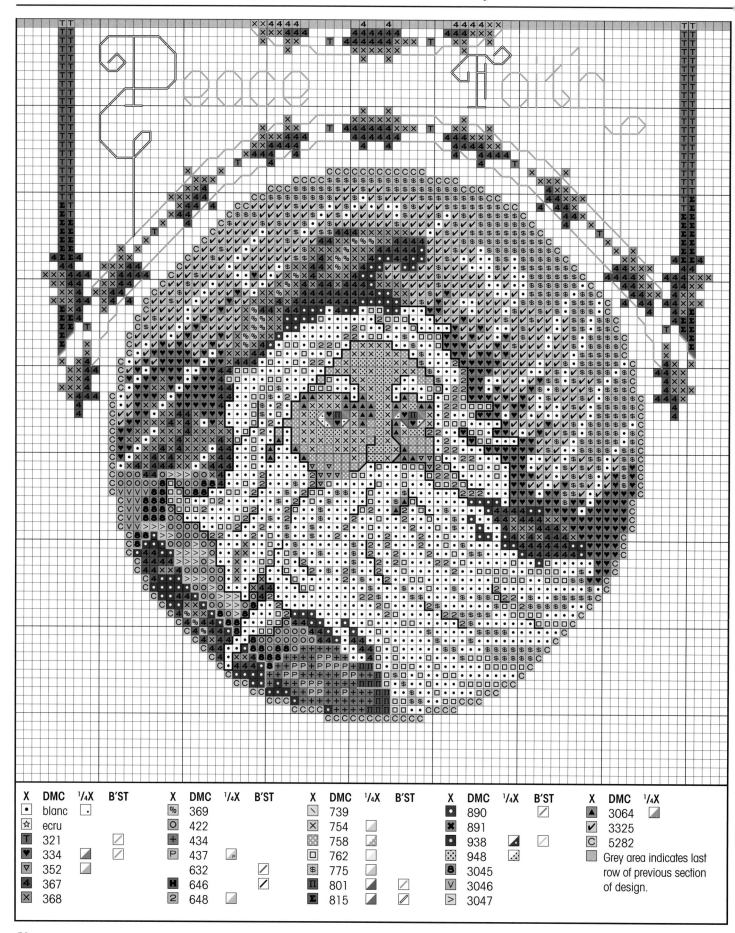

X	DMC	¼X	B'ST		X	DMC	¼X	B'ST		X	DMC	¼X	B'ST		X	DMC	¼X	B'ST		X	DMC	¼X
•	blanc	•			%	369				\	739				●	890		◢		▲	3064	◪
☆	ecru				O	422				X	754	◪			X	891				✔	3325	
T	321		◿		+	434				▦	758	◪			●	938	◢	◢		C	5282	
♥	334	◢	◿		P	437	◪			□	762				◫	948	◪			☐	Grey area indicates last
▽	352	◪				632		◿		$	775				❽	3045					row of previous section
4	367				H	646		◿		Π	801		◿		V	3046					of design.
X	368				2	648	◪			Σ	815	◢	◿		>	3047					

FINISHING INSTRUCTIONS

Portraits from the Past Bell Pull (shown on page 14; chart on pages 48-50).

For bell pull, you will need tracing paper, pencil, two 14" x 28" pieces of fabric for bell pull front and back, 50" length of ³/₈"w braid, 68" length of 1¹/₂"w ribbon, 3" x 12¹/₂" piece of fabric for hanging sleeve, 6" tassel, and clear-drying craft glue.

For bell pull pattern, cut a 13" x 27" piece of tracing paper; fold paper in half lengthwise. Referring to **Fig. 1**, measure 6¹/₄" from one short end of paper and draw a diagonal line to corner. Cut along drawn line, unfold pattern and press flat. Center pattern on wrong side of bell pull front; pin in place. Cut fabric ¹/₂" larger than pattern on all sides. Cut backing fabric same size as bell pull front.

For stitched piece pattern, cut a 6¹/₂" x 19" piece of tracing paper; fold paper in half lengthwise. Referring to **Fig. 1**, measure 3¹/₄" from one short end of paper and draw a diagonal line to corner. Cut along drawn line, unfold pattern and press flat. Center pattern on wrong side of stitched piece with point of pattern 2¹/₂" below bottom edge of design; pin in place. Cut out stitched piece.

Fig. 1

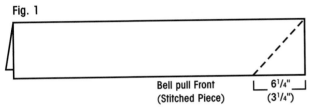

Bell pull Front
(Stitched Piece)   6¹/₄"
                      (3¹/₄")

For bell pull front, refer to photo and center stitched piece on bell pull front; zigzag stitch in place. Beginning at point, glue braid around stitched piece, covering raw edges. Referring to photo, glue ribbon to bell pull front 1" from edges of stitched piece.

Matching right sides and raw edges and leaving an opening for turning, use a ¹/₂" seam allowance to sew backing fabric to bell pull front. Trim corners diagonally; turn bell pull right side out, carefully pushing corners outward. Blind stitch opening closed.

For hanging sleeve, press all edges of fabric ¹/₄" to wrong side; press edges ¹/₄" to wrong side again. Machine stitch pressed edges in place. With one long edge of hanging sleeve ¹/₄" below top of bell pull, center and pin hanging sleeve to bell pull back. Whipstitch long edges of hanging sleeve to bell pull back.

Referring to photo, tack tassel to back of bell pull at point.

Santa Pillow (shown on page 15; chart on page 50).

For pillow, you will need a 17" length of ¹/₈"w braid, 7" square of striped fabric, 30" length of ¹/₄"w braid, two 15" squares of fabric for pillow front and back, 64" length of 3" long purchased fringe with attached seam allowance, polyester fiberfill, and clear-drying craft glue.

Centering design, trim stitched piece to a 4³/₄" dia. circle.

Note: Use a ¹/₂" seam allowance for all seams.

For pillow front, refer to photo and center stitched piece on striped fabric square; zigzag stitch in place. Beginning at bottom center, glue ¹/₈"w braid around stitched piece, covering raw edges. Referring to photo, center stitched piece and striped fabric square on pillow front; zigzag stitch in place. Beginning at bottom point, glue ¹/₄"w braid around striped fabric square, covering raw edges.

For fringe, pin straight edge of fringe to right side of pillow front. Ends of fringe should overlap approximately 2". Baste fringe to pillow front.

Matching right sides and raw edges and leaving an opening for turning, sew pillow front and backing fabric together. Trim seam allowances diagonally at corners; turn pillow right side out, carefully pushing corners outward. Stuff pillow with polyester fiberfill and blind stitch opening closed.

REGAL DELLA ROBBIA

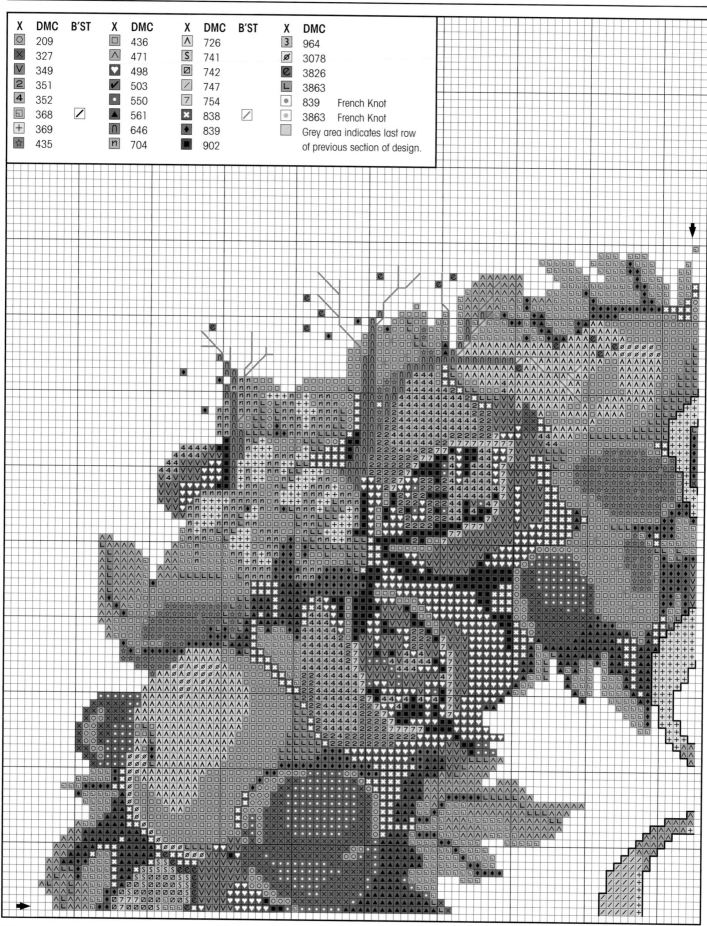

X	DMC	B'ST	X	DMC	X	DMC	B'ST	X	DMC
○	209		□	436	∧	726		3	964
✕	327		∧	471	S	741		∅	3078
∨	349		♥	498	⊠	742		ℓ	3826
2	351		✔	503	╱	747		L	3863
4	352		•	550	7	754		•	839	French Knot
⊡	368	╱	▲	561	✕	838	╱	•	3863	French Knot
+	369		∩	646	◆	839			Grey area indicates last row
☆	435		∩	704	■	902			of previous section of design.

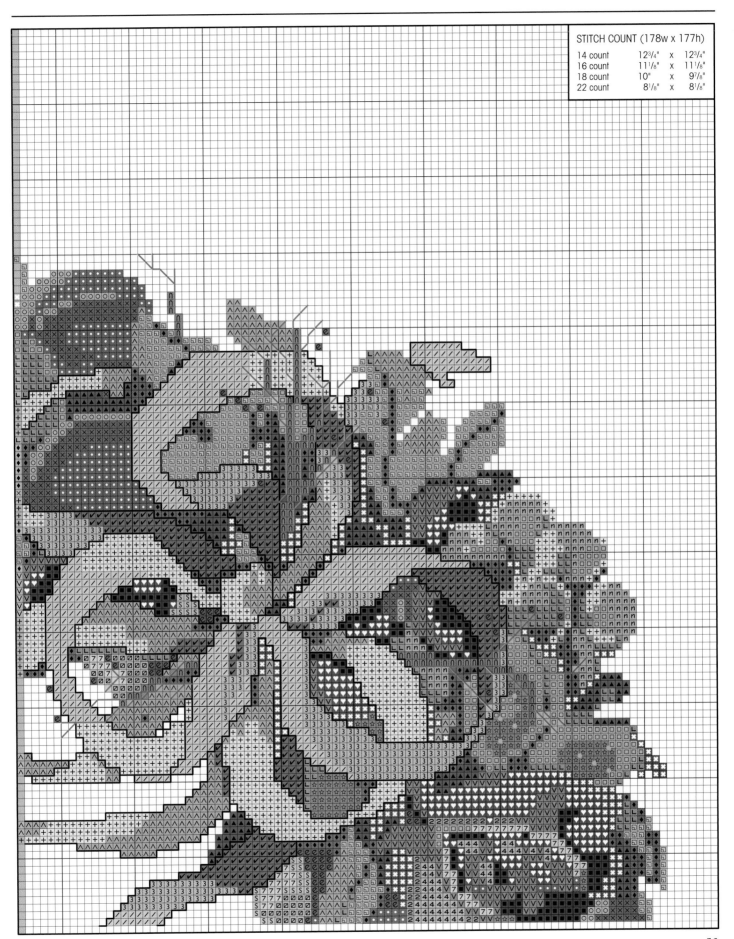

STITCH COUNT (178w x 177h)

14 count	12³/₄"	x	12³/₄"
16 count	11¹/₈"	x	11¹/₈"
18 count	10"	x	9⁷/₈"
22 count	8¹/₈"	x	8¹/₈"

REGAL DELLA ROBBIA

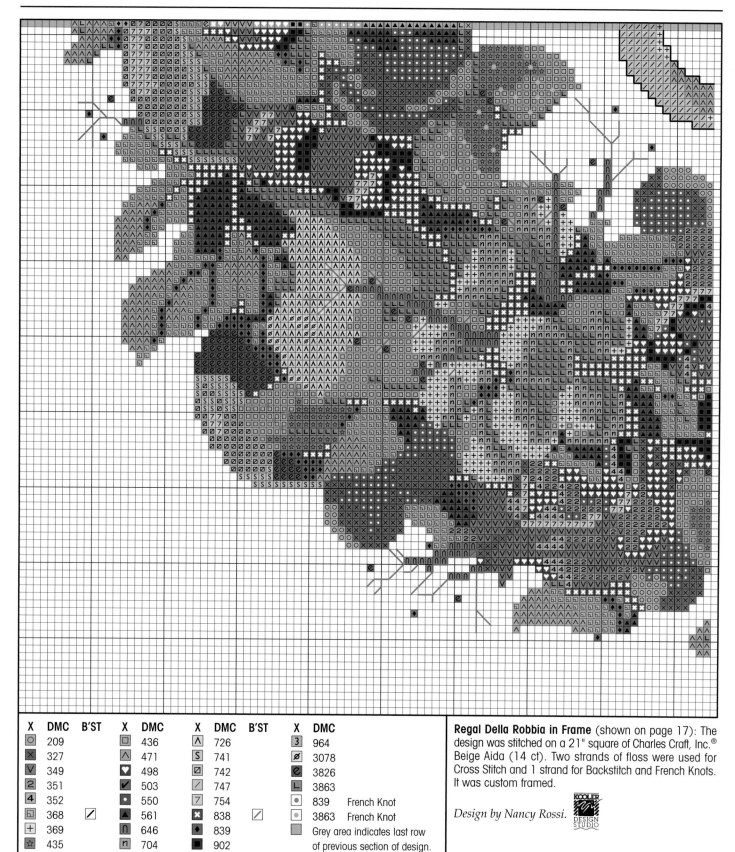

X	DMC	B'ST	X	DMC	X	DMC	B'ST	X	DMC	
○	209		⊡	436	∧	726		③	964	
✕	327		∧	471	S	741		⌀	3078	
V	349		♥	498	⊘	742		e	3826	
2	351		✔	503	⁄	747		L	3863	
4	352		●	550	7	754		●	839	French Knot
⌐	368	⁄	▲	561	✖	838	⁄	○	3863	French Knot
+	369		∩	646	◆	839				Grey area indicates last row
☆	435		n	704	■	902				of previous section of design.

Regal Della Robbia in Frame (shown on page 17): The design was stitched on a 21" square of Charles Craft, Inc.® Beige Aida (14 ct). Two strands of floss were used for Cross Stitch and 1 strand for Backstitch and French Knots. It was custom framed.

Design by Nancy Rossi.

KOOLER DESIGN STUDIO

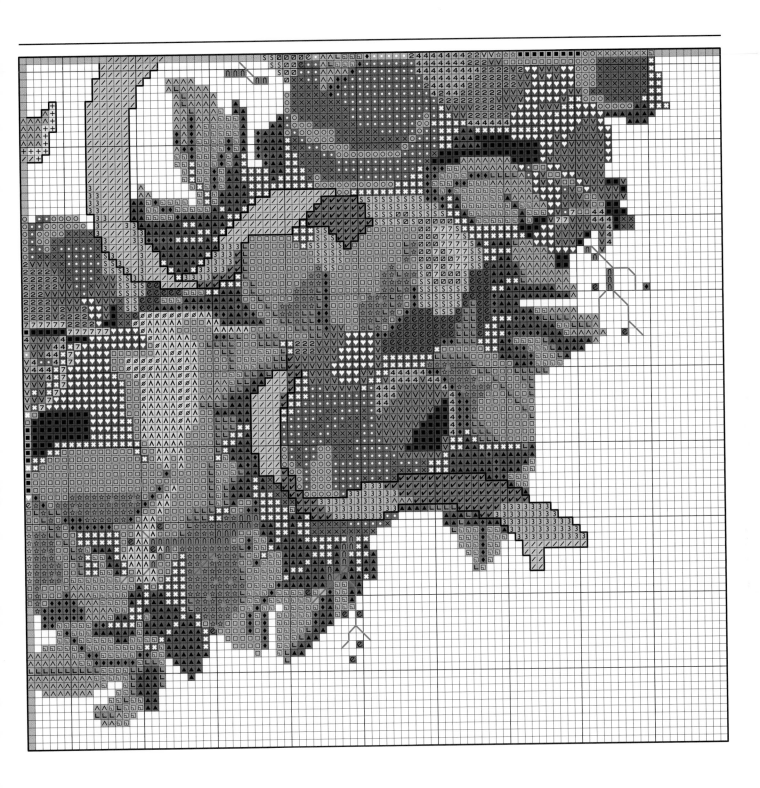

CRIMSON GLORY

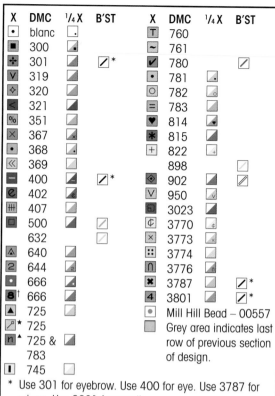

X	DMC	¼ X	B'ST
•	blanc	.	
■	300		
✛	301		╱ *
V	319		
◇	320		
◄	321		
%	351		
✕	367	✕	
•	368	.	
≪	369		
▬	400		╱ *
ℓ	402	ℓ	
⊞	407		
▢	500		╱
	632		╱
▲	640		
2	644	2	
▪	666		
8 †	666		
▲	725		
◢ *	725		
n ▲	725 &		
	783		
▌	745		

X	DMC	¼ X	B'ST
T	760		
~	761		
✔	780		╱
•	781	.	
○	782	○	
═	783		
♥	814	♥	
✳	815		
＋	822	+	
	898		╱
◈	902		╱
V	950	v	
⌐	3023		
¢	3770	¢	
✕	3773		
∷	3774		
∩	3776		
✖	3787		╱ *
4	3801		╱ *
•	Mill Hill Bead – 00557		

Grey area indicates last row of previous section of design.

* Use 301 for eyebrow. Use 400 for eye. Use 3787 for wings. Use 3801 for mouth.

† Use 2 strands of floss and 1 strand of Kreinik Blending Filament – 003HL.

* Use 2 strands of floss and 1 strand of Kreinik Blending Filament – 002HL.

▲ Use 1 strand of each floss color listed and 1 strand of Kreinik Blending Filament – 002HL.

STITCH COUNT (161w x 254h)

14 count	11½"	x	18¼"
16 count	10⅛"	x	15⅞"
18 count	9"	x	14⅛"
22 count	7⅜"	x	11⅝"

Crimson Glory Stocking (shown on pages 18-19): The design was stitched over 2 fabric threads on a 20" x 26" piece of Charles Craft, Inc.® White Monaco (28 ct). Three strands of floss were used for Cross Stitch and 1 strand for Backstitch, unless otherwise noted in the color key. Attach beads using 1 strand of DMC 725 floss. See Attaching Beads, page 96. Personalize stocking using alphabet provided. To complete stocking, see Finishing Instructions, page 77.

"Joy" Hanging Pillow (shown on page 20): Portions of the design (refer to photo) and the word "JOY" from the alphabet were stitched over 2 fabric threads on a 13" x 10" piece of Zweigart® Cream Lugana (25 ct). Three strands of floss were used for Cross Stitch and 1 strand for Backstitch, unless otherwise noted in the color key. To complete pillow, see Finishing Instructions, page 77.

Continued on page 58.

center name

CRIMSON GLORY

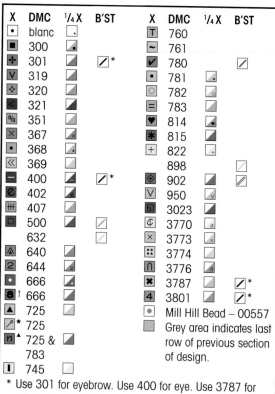

X	DMC	¼X	B'ST	X	DMC	¼X	B'ST
•	blanc			T	760		
■	300			~	761		
✛	301		∕*	✔	780		∕
V	319			•	781		•
◈	320			○	782	○	
◀	321			=	783		
‰	351			♥	814	♥	
✕	367	✕		✳	815		
•	368	•		+	822	+	
≪	369				898		∕
—	400		∕*	◆	902		∕
ℓ	402	ℓ		V	950	√	
⊞	407			◫	3023		
▢	500		∕	¢	3770	¢	
	632		∕	✕	3773	✕	
◭	640			∷	3774		
2	644	2		∩	3776	◹	
◉	666			✖	3787		∕*
❽†	666			4	3801		∕*
▲	725			◉	Mill Hill Bead – 00557		
↗*	725				Grey area indicates last		
n▲	725 &				row of previous section		
	783				of design.		
▯	745						

* Use 301 for eyebrow. Use 400 for eye. Use 3787 for wings. Use 3801 for mouth.

† Use 2 strands of floss and 1 strand of Kreinik Blending Filament – 003HL.

★ Use 2 strands of floss and 1 strand of Kreinik Blending Filament – 002HL.

▲ Use 1 strand of each floss color listed and 1 strand of Kreinik Blending Filament – 002HL.

Poinsettia Candle Band (shown on page 20): A portion of the design (refer to photo) was stitched over 2 fabric threads on a 24" x 8" piece of Zweigart® Cream Lugana (25 ct). Three strands of floss were used for Cross Stitch and 1 strand for Backstitch, unless otherwise noted in the color key. Attach beads using 1 strand of DMC 725 floss. See Attaching Beads, page 96.

For candle band, you will need two 22" lengths of ½"w trim.

Centering design, trim stitched piece to measure 22" x 5½".

Matching right sides and long edges, fold stitched piece in half. Using a ¼" seam allowance, sew long edges together; trim seam allowance to ⅛" and turn stitched piece right side out. With seam centered in back, press stitched piece flat. Referring to photo, sew trim to edges of candle band.

Wrap candle band around candle, turning raw edges to wrong side so that ends meet; blind stitch short ends together.

Christmas Angel in Frame (shown on page 21): A portion of the design (refer to photo) was stitched over 2 fabric threads on a 20" x 18" piece of Zweigart® Cream Lugana (25 ct). Three strands of floss were used for Cross Stitch and 1 strand for Backstitch, unless otherwise noted in the color key. Attach beads using 1 strand of DMC 725 floss. See Attaching Beads, page 96. It was custom framed.

WINTRY RECOLLECTIONS

#5 (39w x 56h)   #6 (39w x 56h)

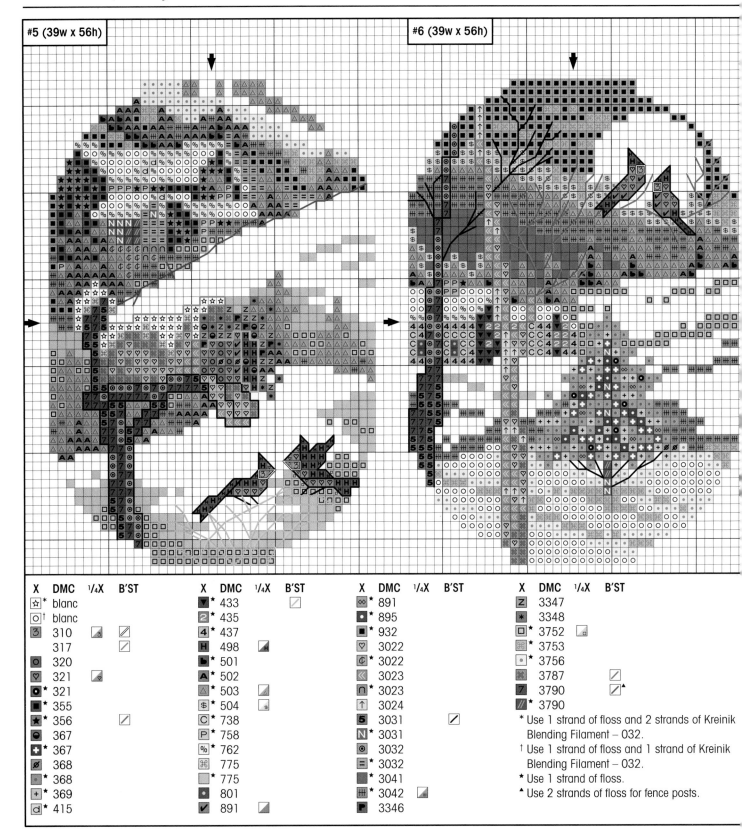

X	DMC	¼X	B'ST		X	DMC	¼X	B'ST		X	DMC	¼X	B'ST		X	DMC	¼X	B'ST
☆*	blanc				▼*	433		◹		∞*	891				⊠	3347		
○†	blanc				▨ 2*	435				◖*	895				✳	3348		
◩ 3	310	◪	◹		▨ 4*	437				■*	932				▫*	3752	◪	
	317		◹		H	498	◢			♡	3022				⊞*	3753		
○	320				▟*	501				¢*	3022				⊡*	3756		
♡	321	◪			A*	502				≪	3023				✕	3787		◹
◉*	321				△*	503		◹		∩*	3023				7	3790		◹^
■*	355				$*	504		◪		↑	3024				⫽*	3790		
★*	356		◹		C*	738				5	3031		◹					
◕	367				P*	758				N*	3031							
⊕*	367				%*	762				◉	3032							
∅	368				⌘	775				=*	3032							
◘*	368				▢	775				◪*	3041							
+*	369				●	801				⊞*	3042	◪						
◩*	415				✔	891		◹		P	3346							

* Use 1 strand of floss and 2 strands of Kreinik
  Blending Filament – 032.
† Use 1 strand of floss and 1 strand of Kreinik
  Blending Filament – 032.
* Use 1 strand of floss.
^ Use 2 strands of floss for fence posts.

O NIGHT DIVINE

X	DMC	¼ X	B'ST
·	blanc	·	
✔	208		
N	210		
↑	301		
■	310		╱
∩	402		
♥	666		
▲	702		
$	704		
A	721		
*	742		
−	744		
↑	754		
×	775		
+	798		
5	799		
◆	840		
¢	841		
Z	958		
○	959		
☆	3607		
T	3609		
H	3820		
╱	3856		

STITCH COUNT (50w x 50h)

14 count	3³⁄₈"	x	3⁵⁄₈"
16 count	3¹⁄₈"	x	3¹⁄₈"
18 count	2⁷⁄₈"	x	2⁷⁄₈"
22 count	2³⁄₈"	x	2³⁄₈"

All project information on page 67.

VISIONS OF OLDE ST. NICK

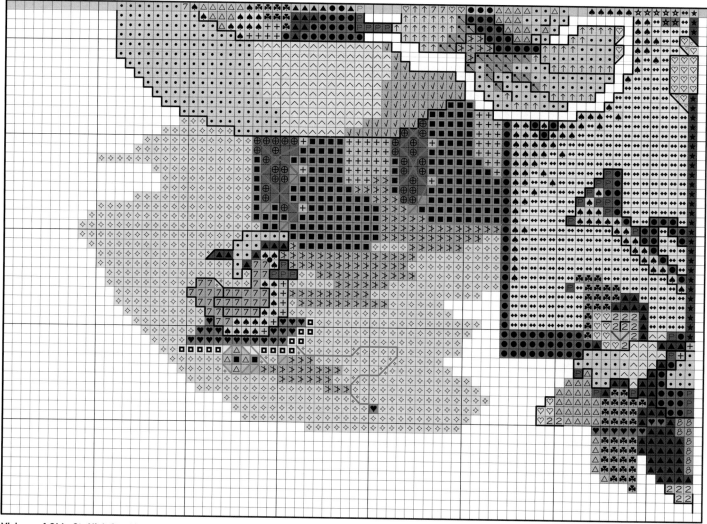

Visions of Olde St. Nick Stocking (shown on pages 24-25): The design was stitched over 2 fabric threads on an 18" x 24" piece of Zweigart® Cream Cashel Linen® (28 ct). Two strands of floss were used for Cross Stitch and 1 strand for Backstitch and French Knots, unless otherwise noted in the color key. Personalize stocking using alphabet provided. To complete stocking, see Finishing Instructions, page 77.

Santa and Sleigh in Frame (shown on page 27): A portion of the design (refer to photo) was stitched over 2 fabric threads on a 13" x 12" piece of Zweigart® Antique White Lugana (25 ct). Three strands of floss were used for Cross Stitch and 1 strand for Backstitch. It was custom framed.

St. Nicholas in Frame (shown on page 29): A portion of the design (refer to photo) was stitched over 2 fabric threads on a 14" x 11" piece of Zweigart® Cream Belfast Linen (32 ct). Two strands of floss were used for Cross Stitch and 1 strand for Backstitch and French Knots. It was custom framed.

Santa Ornament (shown on page 29): A portion of the design (refer to photo) was stitched over 2 fabric threads on an 8" square of Zweigart® Cream

Belfast Linen (32 ct). Two strands of floss were used for Cross Stitch and 1 strand for Backstitch and French Knots.

For ornament, you will need a 6" dia. circle of Cream Belfast Linen for backing, two 4" dia. circles of adhesive mounting board, two 4" dia. circles of batting, 16" length of ¼" dia. purchased cord, and clear-drying craft glue.

Centering design, trim stitched piece to a 6" dia. circle.

Remove paper from one piece of mounting board and press one batting piece onto mounting board. Repeat with remaining mounting board and batting piece.

Clip ³/₈" into edge of stitched piece at ½" intervals. Center stitched piece over batting on one mounting board piece; fold edges of stitched piece to back of mounting board and glue in place. For ornament back, repeat with backing fabric and remaining mounting board. Matching wrong sides, glue ornament front and back together.

Beginning and ending at bottom center of ornament, glue cord around edges of ornament, overlapping ends of cord.

Design by Nancy Rossi.

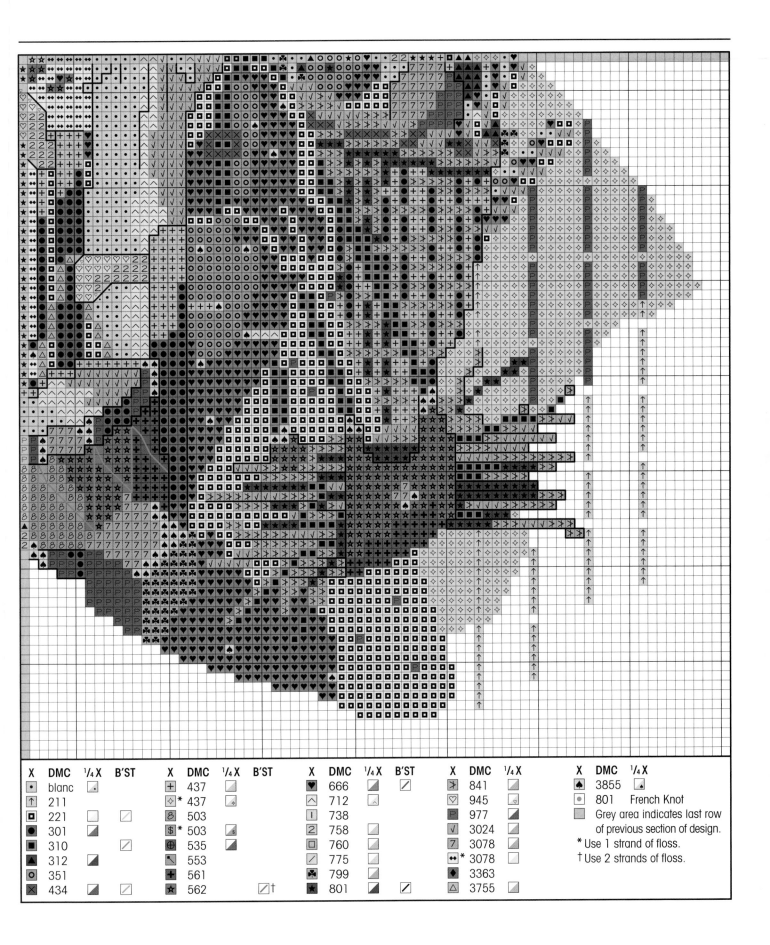

X	DMC	¼X	B'ST		X	DMC	¼X	B'ST		X	DMC	¼X	B'ST		X	DMC	¼X	B'ST		X	DMC	¼X		X	DMC	¼X
•	blanc				+	437				♥	666				⤬	841				♠	3855	
↑	211				✧*	437				∧	712				♡	945				●	801	French Knot
▣	221				8	503				I	738				P	977				▢	Grey area indicates last row
●	301				$*	503				2	758				√	3024				of previous section of design.
■	310				⊕	535				▢	760				7	3078				* Use 1 strand of floss.
▲	312				◥	553				/	775				⤬*	3078				† Use 2 strands of floss.
○	351				✚	561				✖	799				◆	3363				
⤬	434				★	562		†		★	801				△	3755				

73

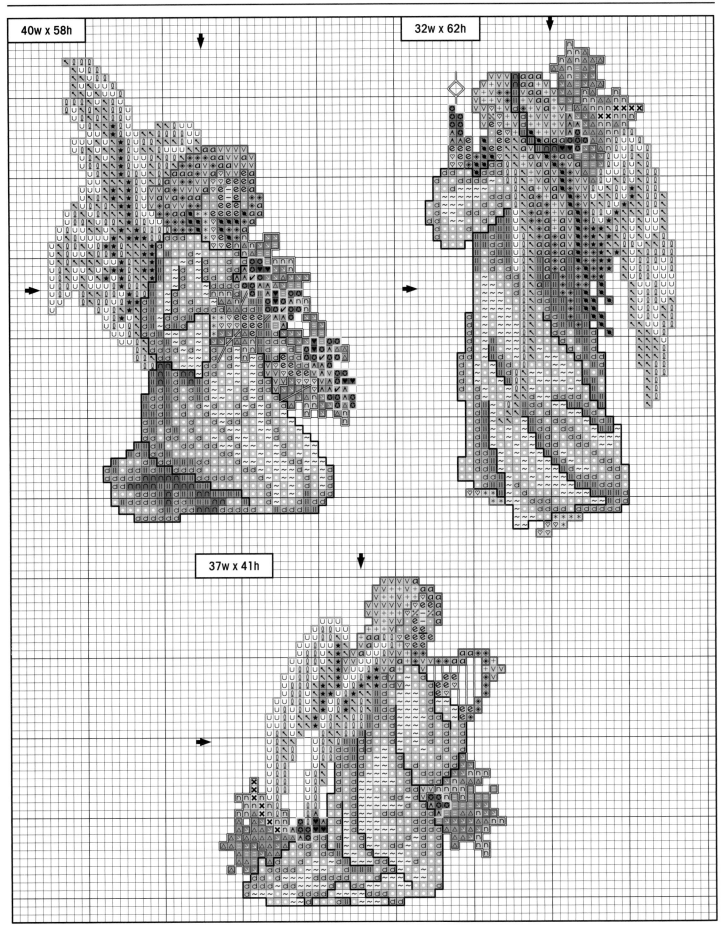

40w x 58h

32w x 62h

37w x 41h

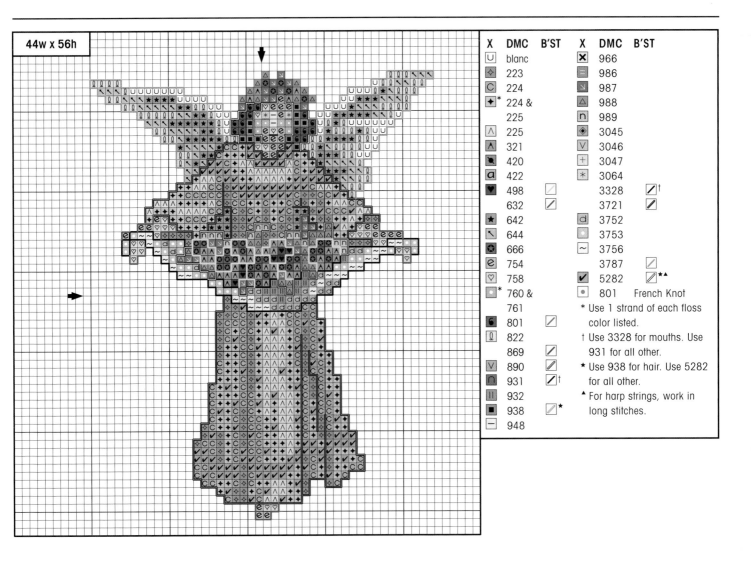

44w x 56h

X	DMC	B'ST	X	DMC	B'ST
U	blanc		✗	966	
◇	223		▤	986	
C	224		↘	987	
✦*	224 &		△	988	
	225		n	989	
∧	225		◈	3045	
▲	321		∨	3046	
◣	420		+	3047	
a	422		*	3064	
▼	498	╱		3328	╱†
	632	╱		3721	╱
★	642		d	3752	
↖	644		▫	3753	
✿	666		~	3756	
e	754			3787	╱
♡	758		✔	5282	╱★▲
▨*	760 &		●	801	French Knot
	761		* Use 1 strand of each floss		
▚	801	╱	color listed.		
◻	822		† Use 3328 for mouths. Use		
	869	╱	931 for all other.		
∨	890	╱	★ Use 938 for hair. Use 5282		
n	931	╱†	for all other.		
‖	932		▲ For harp strings, work in		
◼	938	╱*	long stitches.		
⊟	948				

WINTER VISITORS

FINISHING INSTRUCTIONS

Cardinal and Blue Jay Pillows (shown on page 11, charts on page 46).

For each pillow, you will need two 15" squares of fabric for pillow front and back, 60" length of $^3/_8$" dia. purchased cording with attached seam allowance, 26" length of $^1/_4$" dia. cord with attached tassels, fabric glue, and polyester fiberfill.

Note: Use $^1/_2$" seam allowance for all seams.

Centering design, trim stitched piece to measure $4^1/_2$" square.

For pillow front, center stitched piece on one 15" square of fabric; pin in place. Using a zigzag stitch, machine sew stitched piece to fabric close to raw edges. Referring to photo, tack cord with tassels around outside edge of stitched piece, covering raw edges; tie ends in an overhand knot.

If needed, trim seam allowances of cording to $^1/_2$". Matching raw edges and beginning at bottom center, pin cording to right side of pillow front, making a $^3/_8$" clip in seam allowance of cording at corners. Ends of cording should overlap approximately 4". Turn overlapped ends of cording toward outside edge of pillow front; baste cording to pillow front.

Matching right sides and raw edges, pin pillow front and backing fabric together. Leaving an opening for turning, sew pillow front and backing fabric together. Trim seam allowances diagonally at corners; turn pillow right side out, carefully pushing corners outward. Stuff pillow with polyester fiberfill and blind stitch opening closed.

father christmas

X	DMC	¼ X	B'ST
<	311		
(	320		
▲	347		⁄ *†
L	350		⁄ *†
◇ ★	351 &		
	352		
♡ ★	351 &		
	760		
✔ ★	352 &		
	761		
▬	433		
↑	435		
+	437		
✳	501		⁄ △
S	502		
8	611		
⬚°	611		
⊠ ★	612 &		
	613		
◾	645		⁄
2	647		
3	648		
⊕ ★	676 &		
	743		
•|•	721		
H ★	741 &		
	977		
Y	745		
6	746		⁄ *†
C	758		
➕ ★	807 &		
	932		
▣	815		
◉	844		⁄
◼	898		⁄
	898		⁄ *
⦁	932		
△	945		
n	951		
≪ ★	989 &		
	3348		
‰	3045		
7	3047		
◇	3064		
4	3072		
◼	3371		⁄ △
✕	3752		
⊕ ★	3752 &		
	3766		
═	3760		⁄ △
	3760		⁄ *
◆	3772		⁄
>	3811		
•	3865		
◒	5282		
◉	350	French Knot	
●	898	French Knot	
O	Charm Placement.		

Grey area indicates last row of previous section of design.

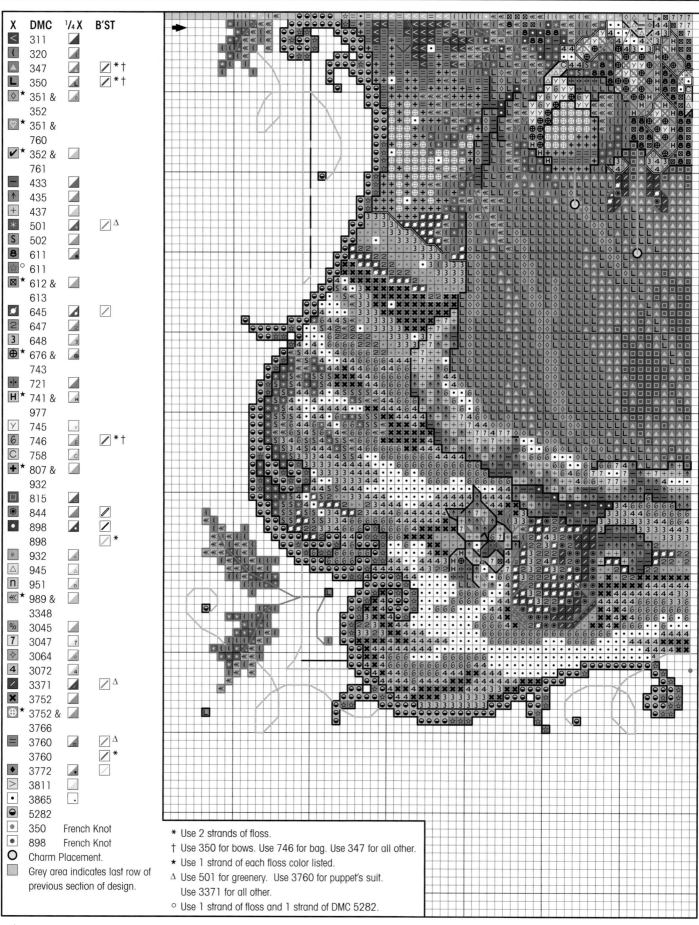

* Use 2 strands of floss.

† Use 350 for bows. Use 746 for bag. Use 347 for all other.

★ Use 1 strand of each floss color listed.

△ Use 501 for greenery. Use 3760 for puppet's suit. Use 3371 for all other.

° Use 1 strand of floss and 1 strand of DMC 5282.

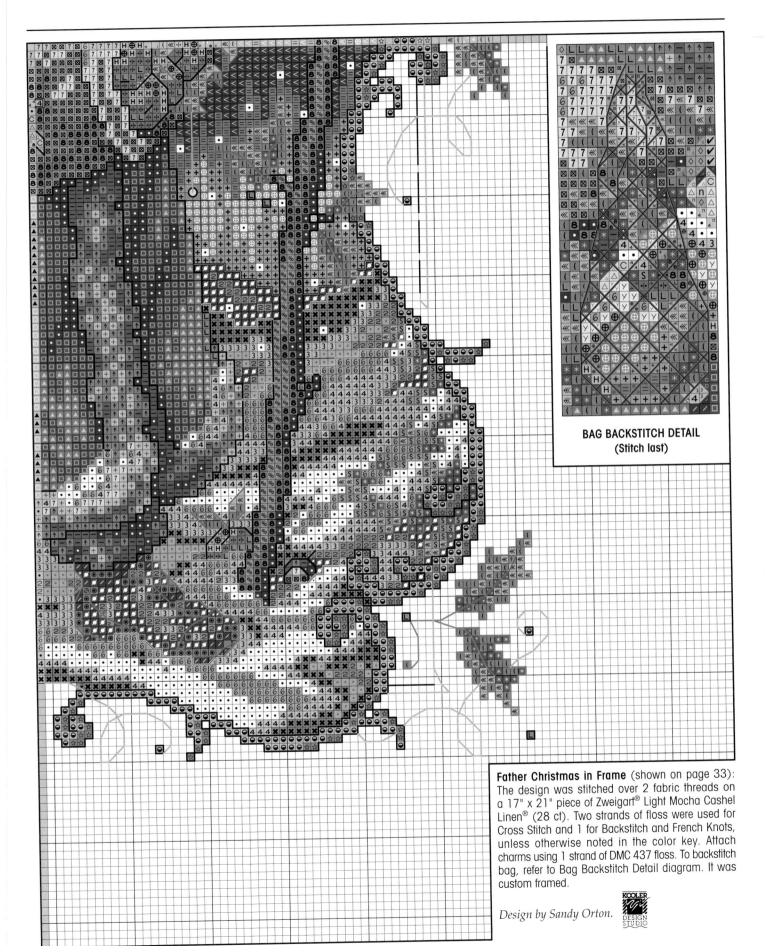

BAG BACKSTITCH DETAIL
(Stitch last)

Father Christmas in Frame (shown on page 33):
The design was stitched over 2 fabric threads on
a 17" x 21" piece of Zweigart® Light Mocha Cashel
Linen® (28 ct). Two strands of floss were used for
Cross Stitch and 1 for Backstitch and French Knots,
unless otherwise noted in the color key. Attach
charms using 1 strand of DMC 437 floss. To backstitch
bag, refer to Bag Backstitch Detail diagram. It was
custom framed.

Design by Sandy Orton.

KOOLER
DESIGN
STUDIO

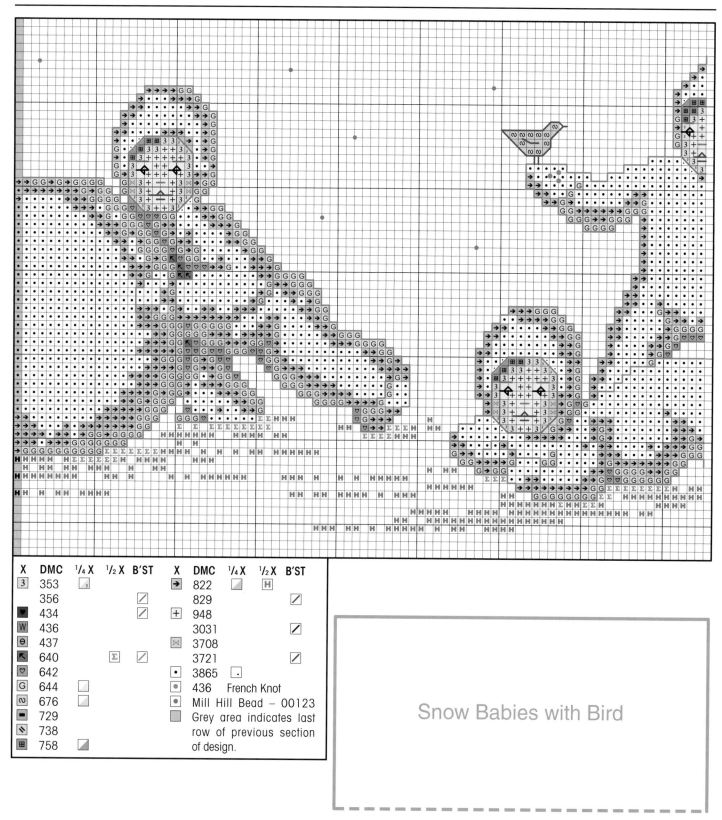

X	DMC	¼ X	½ X	B'ST	X	DMC	¼ X	½ X	B'ST
3	353	3			→	822		H	
	356		/			829			/
♥	434		/		+	948			
W	436					3031			/
θ	437				⋈	3708			
K	640		Σ	/		3721			/
♡	642				•	3865	·		
G	644	◹			●	436	French Knot		
∾	676	◹			●	Mill Hill Bead – 00123			
▪	729				▨	Grey area indicates last row of previous section of design.			
⧄	738								
⊞	758	◹							

Snow Babies with Bird

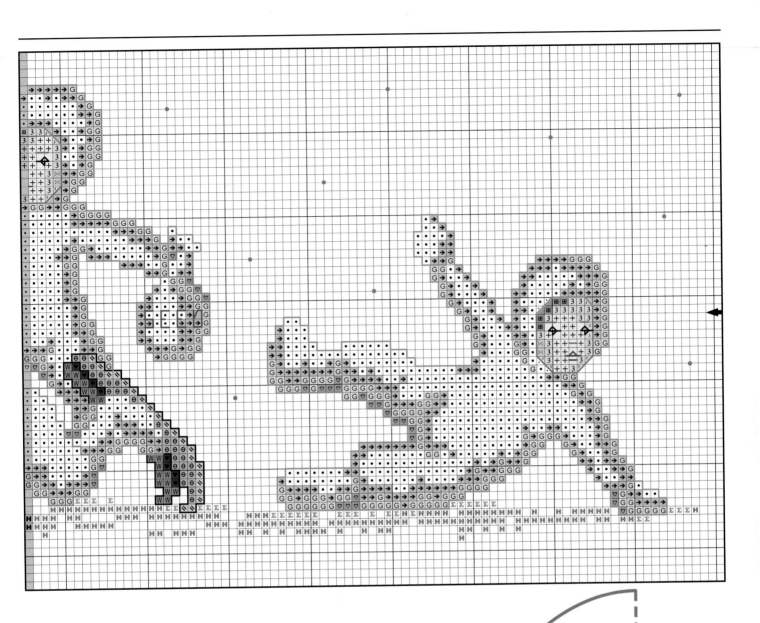

Sledders
Snow Baby with Snowball

Snow Baby
with Stars

SANTA'S FOREST FRIENDS

X	DMC	¼X	B'ST	X	DMC	¼X	B'ST	X	DMC	¼X	B'ST	X	DMC	¼X	B'ST	X	DMC	¼X	½X	B'ST
•	blanc		◢*	☒	369 &			6	647	◢			801	◢		|||	842			
▼†	221 &	◢			747			⊙†	738 &		◢*	T	822	⊤		▷	948	▷		
	902			◢	407	◢			739			⊙	838	◢		8	989	◢		
2†	223 &	◢		⊟†	420 &			✦	754	✦			839		◢	☒	3023	☒	◖	
	3833				3828			√	758	◢		4†	839 &	◢		=*	3023	☒		
✖	319	◢		◢	422	◢		◤	760 &	◢			840			∎	3371	◢		◢
▼	367	◢		❚	433				761			∎	840			★†	3721 &	◢		
↑†	368 &	◢			535		◢	z	761	z		◆†	841 &				3831			
	3348			∎	644	◢			791		◢*		842							

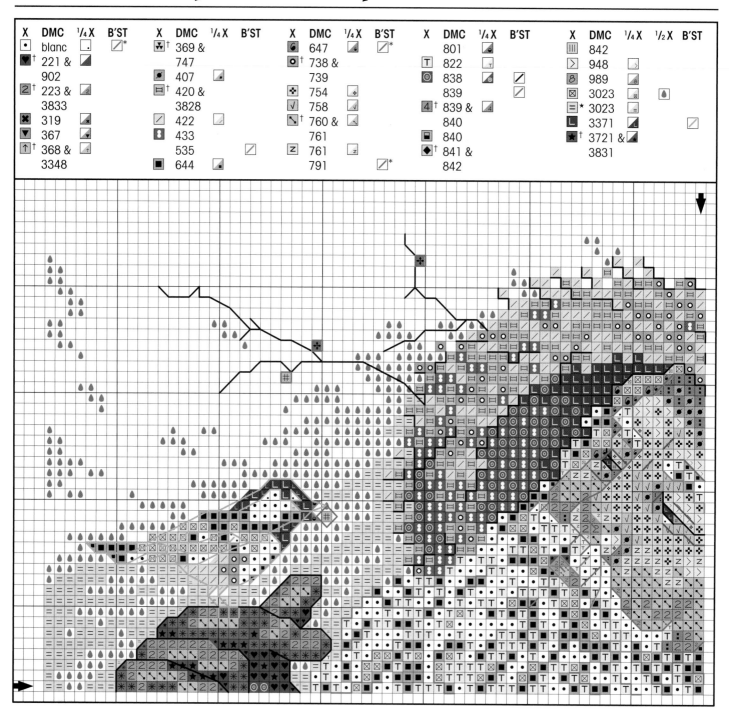

X	DMC	¼X	B'ST
✱†	3722 & 3832	◹	
⦂	3772	◹	◹
✚	3807		
⊞	3839	◹	
▣	3840		
●	blanc	French Knot	
▨	Grey area indicates last row of previous section of design.		

* Use 647 for beard and eyebrows. Use 791 for berries. Use blanc for all other.

† Use 1 strand of each floss color listed.

* Use 1 strand of floss.

Santa's Forest Friends in Frame (shown on page 41): The design was stitched over 2 fabric threads on a 17" x 14" piece of Zweigart® Platinum Cashel Linen® (28 ct). Two strands of floss were used for Cross Stitch and 1 strand for Half Cross Stitch, Backstitch, and French Knot, unless otherwise noted in the color key. It was inserted in a frame courtesy of East Side Mouldings (14¼ x 12 – 2200AO).

Design by Sandi Gore Evans.
Needlework adaptation
by Sandy Orton.

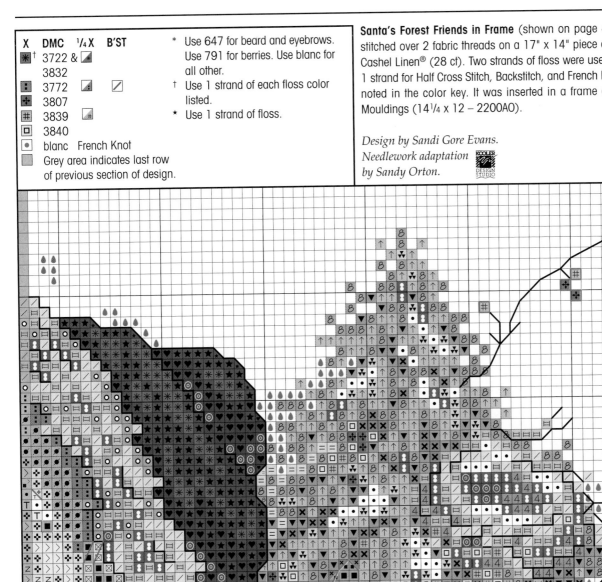

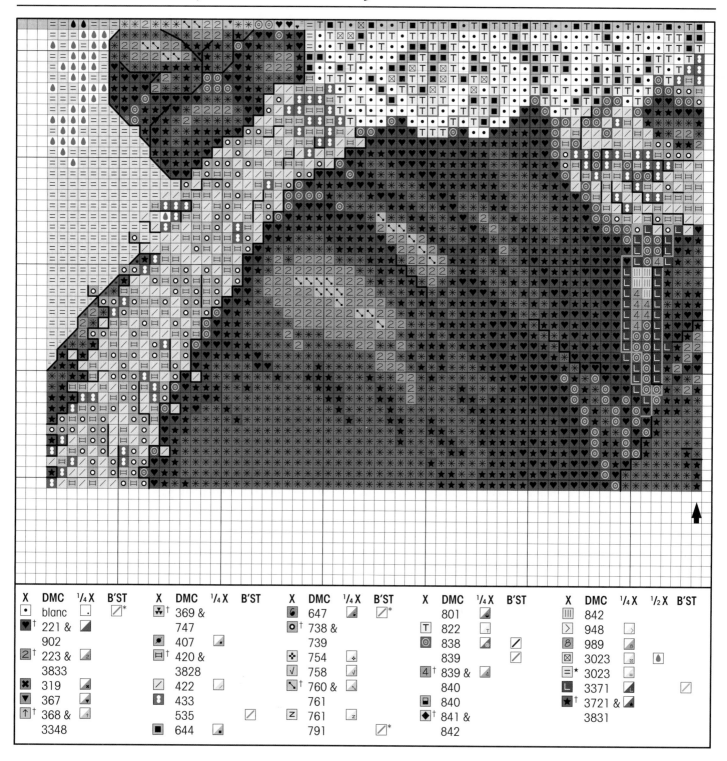

X	DMC	¼ X	B'ST		X	DMC	¼ X	B'ST		X	DMC	¼ X	B'ST		X	DMC	¼ X	B'ST		X	DMC	¼ X	½ X	B'ST
•	blanc		*		▼†	369 &				6	647		*			801				‖‖‖	842			
▼†	221 &					747				○†	738 &				T	822	T			>	948	>		
	902				●	407					739				◎	838				8	989			
2†	223 &				⊟†	420 &				✢	754	✦				839				⊠	3023		⬤	
	3833					3828				√	758					839 &				=★	3023			
✖	319				╱	422				↘†	760 &				4†	840				L	3371			
▼	367				8	433					761				■	840				★†	3721 &			
↑†	368 &					535				z	761	z			◆†	841 &					3831			
	3348				■	644					791		*			842								

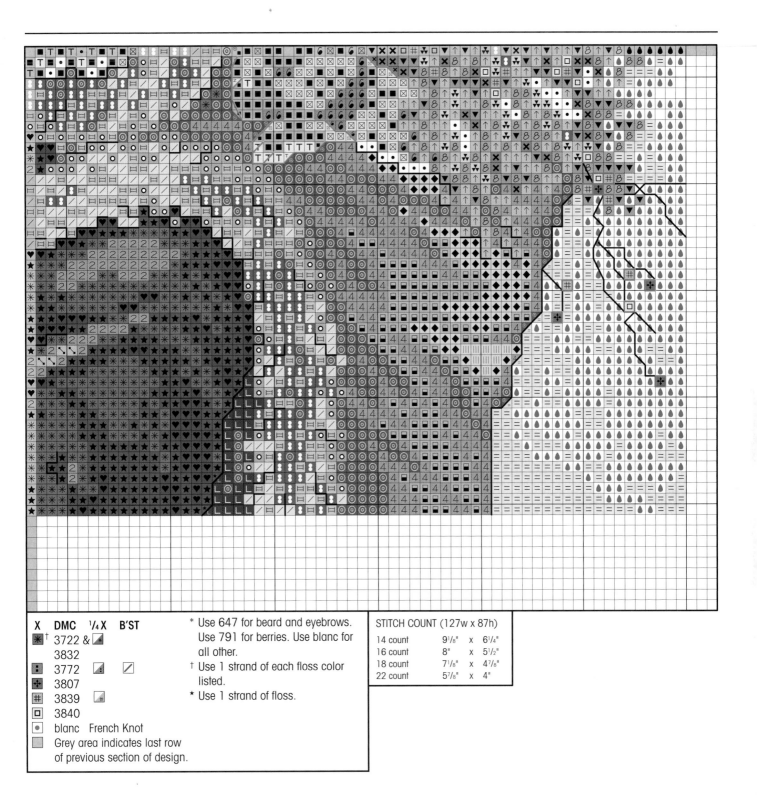

X	DMC	1/4 X	B'ST
✳†	3722 &	◣	
	3832		
⦂	3772	◢	╱
✛	3807		
⌗	3839	◢	
▣	3840		
•	blanc	French Knot	
▨	Grey area indicates last row of previous section of design.		

* Use 647 for beard and eyebrows. Use 791 for berries. Use blanc for all other.
† Use 1 strand of each floss color listed.
* Use 1 strand of floss.

STITCH COUNT (127w x 87h)

count			
14 count	9 1/8"	x	6 1/4"
16 count	8"	x	5 1/2"
18 count	7 1/8"	x	4 7/8"
22 count	5 7/8"	x	4"

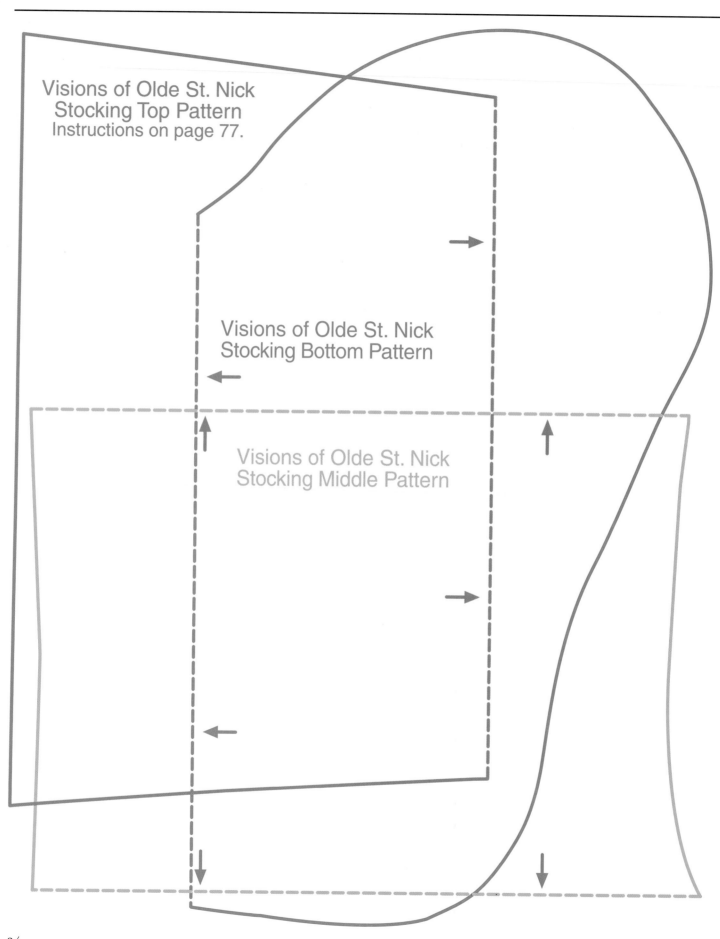

Visions of Olde St. Nick
Stocking Top Pattern
Instructions on page 77.

Visions of Olde St. Nick
Stocking Bottom Pattern

Visions of Olde St. Nick
Stocking Middle Pattern

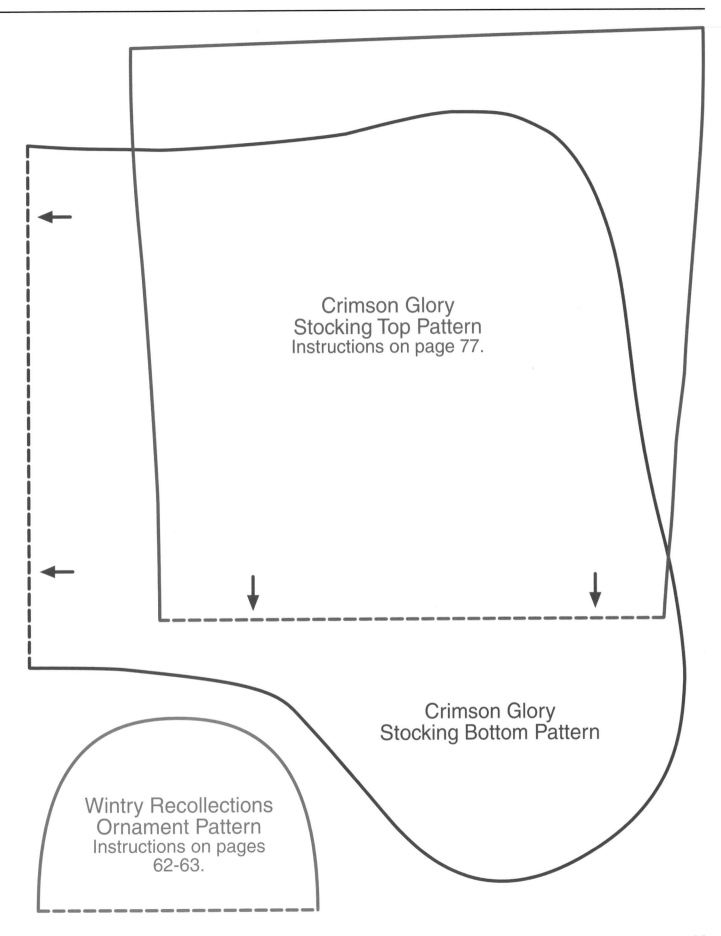

Crimson Glory
Stocking Top Pattern
Instructions on page 77.

Crimson Glory
Stocking Bottom Pattern

Wintry Recollections
Ornament Pattern
Instructions on pages
62-63.

GENERAL INSTRUCTIONS

WORKING WITH CHARTS

How to Read Charts: Each of the designs is shown in chart form. Each colored square on the chart represents one Cross Stitch or one Half Cross Stitch. Each colored triangle on the chart represents one Quarter Stitch. In some charts, reduced symbols are used to indicate Quarter Stitches (**Fig. 1**). **Fig. 2** and **Fig. 3** indicate Cross Stitch under Backstitch.

Fig. 1	Fig. 2	Fig. 3
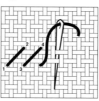

Black or colored dots on the chart represent Cross Stitch, French Knots, or bead placement. The black or colored straight lines on the chart indicate Backstitch. The symbol is omitted or reduced when a French Knot, Backstitch, or bead covers a square.

Each chart is accompanied by a color key. This key indicates the color of floss to use for each stitch on the chart. The headings on the color key are for Cross Stitch (**X**), DMC color number (**DMC**), Quarter Stitch (**¼X**), Half Cross Stitch (**½X**), and Backstitch (**B'ST**). Color key columns should be read vertically and horizontally to determine type of stitch and floss color. Some designs may include stitches worked with metallic thread, such as blending filament. The metallic thread may be blended with floss or used alone. If any metallic thread is used in a design, the color key will contain the necessary information.

STITCHING TIPS

Attaching Beads: Refer to chart for bead placement and sew bead in place using a fine needle that will pass through bead. Bring needle up at 1, run needle through bead and then down at 2. Secure floss on back or move to next bead as shown in **Fig. 4**.

Fig. 4

Working over Two Fabric Threads: Use the sewing method instead of the stab method when working over two fabric threads. To use the sewing method, keep your stitching hand on the right side of the fabric (instead of stabbing the fabric with the needle and taking your stitching hand to the back of the fabric to pick up the needle). With the sewing method, you take the needle down and up with one stroke instead of two. To add support to stitches, it is important that the first Cross Stitch be placed on the fabric with stitch 1-2 beginning and ending where a

vertical fabric thread crosses over a horizontal fabric thread (**Fig. 5**). When the first stitch is in the correct position, the entire design will be placed properly, with vertical fabric threads supporting each stitch.

Fig. 5

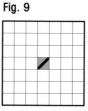

STITCH DIAGRAMS

Note: Bring threaded needle up at 1 and all odd numbers and down at 2 and all even numbers.

Counted Cross Stitch (X): Work one Cross Stitch to correspond to each colored square on the chart. For horizontal rows, work stitches in two journeys (**Fig. 6**). For vertical rows, complete each stitch as shown (**Fig. 7**). When working over two fabric threads, work Cross Stitch as shown in **Fig. 8**. When the chart shows a Backstitch crossing a colored square (**Fig. 9**), a Cross Stitch should be worked first; then the Backstitch (**Fig. 14** or **15**) should be worked on top of the Cross Stitch.

Fig. 6	Fig.7

Fig. 8	Fig. 9
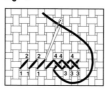

Quarter Stitch (¼X): Quarter Stitches are denoted by triangular shapes of color on the chart and on the color key. For a Quarter Stitch, come up at 1 (**Fig. 10**), then split fabric thread to go down at 2. **Fig. 11** shows the technique for Quarter Stitches when working over two fabric threads.

Fig. 10	Fig. 11

Half Cross Stitch (½X): This stitch is one journey of the Cross Stitch and is worked from lower left to upper right as shown in **Fig. 12**. When working over two fabric threads, work Half Cross Stitch as shown in **Fig. 13**.

Fig. 12	Fig. 13
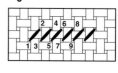

Backstitch (B'ST): For outline detail, Backstitch (shown on chart and on color key by black or colored straight lines) should be worked after the design has been completed (**Fig. 14**). When working over two fabric threads, work Backstitch as shown in **Fig. 15**.

Fig. 14	Fig. 15

French Knot: Bring needle up at 1. Wrap floss once around needle and insert needle at 2, holding end of floss with non-stitching fingers (**Fig. 16**). Tighten knot, then pull needle through fabric, holding floss until it must be released. For larger knot, use more strands of floss; wrap only once.

Fig. 16

Photo models were stitched using DMC floss, courtesy of The DMC Corporation.

Instructions tested and photo items made by Kandi Ashford, Muriel Hicks, Pat Johnson, Patricia O'Neil, Stephanie Gail Sharp, Lavonne Sims, and Trish Vines.